THE TRUTH ABOUT
CROCODILES

Maxwell Eaton III

ROARING BROOK PRESS

NEW YORK

Copyright © 2019 by Maxwell Eaton III
Published by Roaring Brook Press
Roaring Brook Press is a division of Holtzbrinck
Publishing Holdings Limited Partnership
175 Fifth Avenue, New York, NY 10010
The art for this book was created using pen and ink with digital coloring.
mackids.com

ISBN: 978-1-250-19844-0
Library of Congress Control Number: 2018956033

Our books may be purchased in bulk for promotional, educational, or business use. Please
contact your local bookseller or the Macmillan Corporate and Premium Sales Department
at (800) 221-7945 ext. 5442 or by e-mail at MacmillanSpecialMarkets@macmillan.com.

First edition, 2019
Book design by Jennifer Browne

Printed in China by Shaoguan Fortune Creative Industries Co. Ltd.,
Shaoguan, Guangdong Province

1 3 5 7 9 10 8 6 4 2

For
EEE

These are crocodilians (croc-o-DILL-ee-ans). Some people call all of them crocodiles. We'll call them crocs.

CROCS CAN BE FOUND IN TROPICAL AND SUBTROPICAL WETLANDS, RIVERS, PONDS, LAKES, AND COASTLINES ALL ACROSS THE WORLD.

There are three croc families.
Here's how to tell them apart.

Crocodiles

Habitat: Saltwater and freshwater wetlands, rivers, lakes, and coasts

Alligators and Caimans

Habitat: Freshwater wetlands, streams, rivers, and lakes

The Gharial (GAR-ee-all)

Habitat: Large rivers in southeast Asia

All crocs are reptiles, like turtles, snakes, and lizards.

COLD-BLOODED ANIMALS DON'T BURN ENERGY TO STAY WARM, LIKE HUMANS DO. INSTEAD, THEY DEPEND ON THE WARMTH OF THE WATER, AIR, AND GROUND AROUND THEM.

Crocs can walk and run on land, but they're most at home in the water.

CROCS OFTEN KEEP SMALL ROCKS IN THEIR STOMACHS. ONE THEORY IS THAT IT ALLOWS THEM TO KEEP MORE AIR IN THEIR LUNGS WITHOUT FLOATING, SO THEY CAN STAY UNDERWATER FOR LONGER.

My dentist is furious.

They can hear, see, and breathe above water while floating.

Ears

Eyes

Nostrils

Someone's nose is whistling.

Crocs can rest underwater for hours.

Some female crocs lay eggs in mounds built out of grass, leaves, and mud. The mother lays them at night and then covers them up using her hind feet.

Many creatures enjoy a tasty croc egg, so the mother may guard the mound until the eggs hatch two to three months later.

When the baby crocs are ready to hatch, they make *mew* sounds like kittens until their mother digs them out.

American alligator hatchling—6 to 8 inches long

The mother will then carry them in her mouth to a safe place in the water. She may watch over them for almost two years!

A BABY CROC OFTEN WEIGHS AS LITTLE AS A STICK OF BUTTER.

They may start life small,
but some crocs grow large.

And large crocs need lots of food.

THE SMALLEST CROCS ARE THE CUVIER'S DWARF CAIMAN AND THE AFRICAN DWARF CROCODILE. BOTH REACH ABOUT FIVE FEET IN LENGTH.

Hunting takes patience. Crocs will float silently, like a log, watching for an animal to approach the water's edge.

Crocs have lots of teeth, but they don't actually chew. Instead, the teeth grip the prey while the croc rolls wildly and whips its head around to tear the food into pieces it can swallow.

Once inside the croc's stomach, acid breaks down the meal—bones, beaks, claws, quills, feathers, fur, and all!

Many crocs are dangerous, but there are ways to avoid being a piñata when traveling in croc country.

But you can help by reading about crocs and then teaching others. Because crocs are magnificent animals!

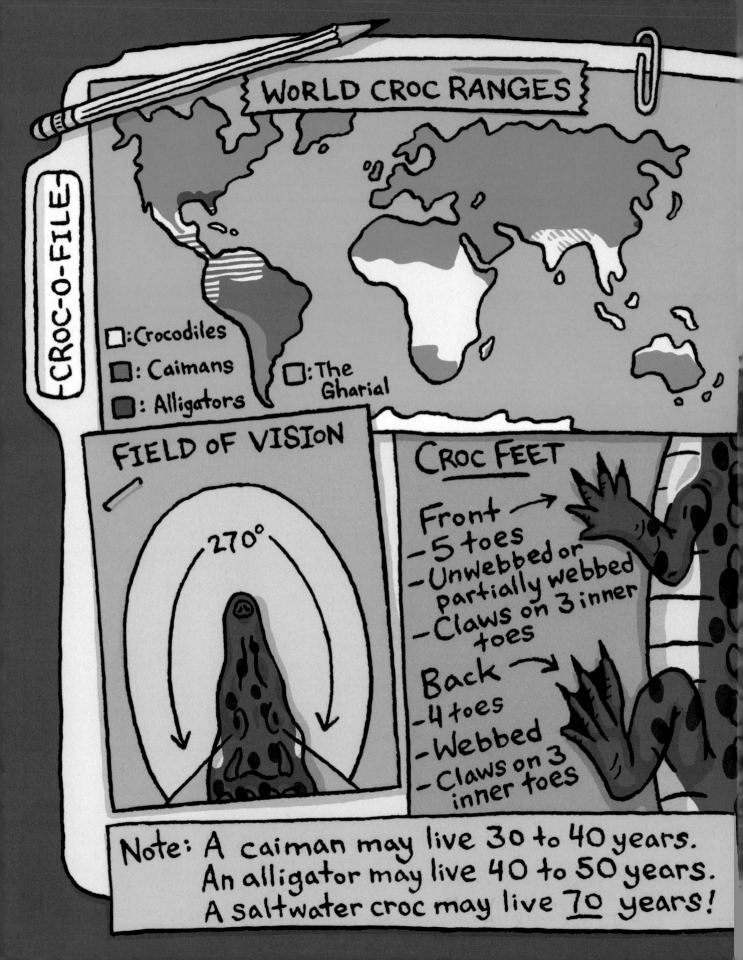

American and Chinese alligators often rest in underground dens in the winter.

Z

Found noise-maker (?)

Inside the egg

Subaudible vibrations (SAVs)
- special calls that travel far underwater
- so low-pitched that humans can't hear them
- makes water "dance" over the alligator's back

↑ American alligator

Further Research

DWARF CROCODILE-SIZED BOOKS

Alligators and Crocodiles!, Laurence Pringle, illustrated by Meryl Henderson, Boyds Mills Press, 2009.

Supercroc and the Origin of Crocodiles, Christopher Sloan, National Geographic, 2002.

SALTWATER CROCODILE-SIZED BOOKS

Biology and Evolution of Crocodylians, Gordon Grigg, illustrated by David Kirshner, Comstock, 2015.

Reptiles and Amphibians, Mark O'Shea and Tim Halliday, DK, 2001.